PLANT CONSCIOUSNESS, PLANT CARE

Also by Shirley Ross

THE INTERIOR ECOLOGY COOKBOOK

PLANT CONSCIOUSNESS, PLANT CARE

SHIRLEY ROSS

Illustrations by
Beth Cannon

QUADRANGLE
The New York Times Book Company

TO JOHNNY AND MR. Z

Library of Congress Catalog Card Number: 37-79931
International Standard Book Number: 0-8129-0394-3

INTERIOR DESIGN BY BETTY BINNS

PLANT CONSCIOUSNESS

In ancient times men and women lived amongst the plants and trees. Vegetation was their physical environment and their source of sustenance. No wonder that our ancestors responded to the plants as beings with souls of their own and revered the energy within them as divine.

Today we exist in a devegetated concrete and cement environment. Where once we lived in the forests and worshiped the plants as gods, the best we can do now is to make some small attempt to communicate with them by enriching our dwelling places with house plants.

This is a book about caring for house plants. But a prerequisite for any such attempt must involve an understanding not only of what plants mean, to us now, but the part they have played in the development of our spirituality and consciousness. Recent scientific revelations indicate that plants have emotions and feel things in much the same way as humans. There also is evidence that plant perceptions are communicated through strange signals that are yet beyond our realm of awareness.

Though we find these developments startling, they would not be surprising to people of more primitive times who lived in daily contact with the wisdom of plants. Part One of this book—Plant Consciousness—presents both the recent scientific developments and the history and background of the spiritual relationship between people and plants. Part Two—Plant Care—is the planet-side version of this scientific-spiritual overview: the day-to-day activity and communication of living with plants—the ultimate "plant consciousness."

3

ASK AND EMBLA

According to the legends, after the creation of heaven
and earth, the Germanic god Odin and his brothers
came upon two trees, while walking by the sea, and
changed them into human beings, one male and the
other female. From the first brother they received life
and soul; from the second, wit and the will to move;
from the third, face, speech, sight, and hearing. The
gods also gave them clothing and chose their names.
Ask was the man's name, and Embla the woman's.
And thus did they create man and woman. From
the ash, Ask, the first man, was made; from the elm,
Embla, the first woman.

IN THE BEGINNING

In the beginning the trees were worshiped as gods. Plant worship, the first form of religion, predates all recorded history. Our primitive ancestors lived in an endless forest of trees, trees as far as the eye could see, as far as the mind could imagine, oceans of trees, a vast unknown and feared horizon. This plant life was central to both physical sustenance and spiritual realities; it was believed that spirits inhabited and animated the trees and plants, that they suffered and died with them. The story of the birth of man and woman in the Ask and Embla legend was common knowledge to people on all five continents of the world thousands of years before Darwin propounded his theory of evolution, thousands of years before the creation of Adam and Eve.

WORSHIP IN THE GROVE

We believe in our plants. We feel instinctive friendship toward them. Perhaps it has been in our blood since the days when our ancestors worshiped in the groves. Primitive people were born into forests which they had no part in planting and which they barely understood. They must have realized that the varied life of plants existed long before there were human eyes to watch it, human minds to wonder at it, and human brains and hands to modify it. We have ignored this ancient wisdom and treated our plants as mere objects, divorcing them from the spiritual part of our existence. We think only of what they mean to us now, not what they meant in the past. We do not honor their rightful place in our human hearts and memory. How strange for us to think that the plants we value now only for beauty and grace were once worshiped as gods.

8

YGGDRASIL

Myths relating to plant worship are the origins of many interesting cosmologies of the universe. The story of Yggdrasil, an imaginary tree, predates by centuries the first scientific ideas of the cosmos. This imaginary tree was believed to bear up the heaven above the earth. The Babylonians placed it near Eridu, an ancient city near the mouth of the Euphrates. Its roots grew deep in the watery abyss, the dwelling of the amphibious Ea, god of wisdom, who supplied the springs and rivers that fertilized the earth. On the leaves rested Zikum, the primeval mother, the heaven from which all things have come. Earth was midway between the roots of the tree and its topmost branches. In its stem dwelt the earth mother, her consort Dovkina, and her son Tammuz, the sun god, to whom was wedded Istar, the Astarte of the Syrians, the Aphrodite of the Greeks, the Venus of the Romans. Yggdrasil was an ash, the same tree from which Ask, the first man, came forth. Yggdrasil: tree of existence, of life, and of knowledge, sorrow and fate; the source of all things, including time and space. Yggdrasil: the upholder of the universe.

We modern humans live in immaculate physical environments. The dirt floors from which living things grow were covered over long ago. The best we can do to ease our anxious hunger for things green and alive is to live amongst the few plants we welcome into our homes. We study our plants and see in them a special awareness that complements our aggressive human nature. Plants are passive, subjectively contemplative, and devoutly acquiescent. They simply spread their leaves and absorb directly the essential elixir of life, which we as humans receive secondhand in the harvest of our plants or the mangled flesh of our animals. Our plants maintain immediate physical contact with the source of all cosmic being—a physical state, but also a spiritual one.

WHAT YOU ARE

The poets will not let us forget. They ponder the wisdom hidden in plants, the key to identity found in flowers.

Flower in the crannied wall,
I pluck you out of the crannies,
I hold you here, root and all, in my hand,
Little flower—but if I could understand
What you are, root and all, and all in all,
I should know what God and man is.

                                                  TENNYSON

THE APPEAL OF THE PLANTS

In many lands ancient races worshiped and showed obeisance to trees, plants, and their flowers. In their worship of plants is found an expression of the spirituality of plants, an answer to the demand from within, the desire to commune with a mysterious, universal being. This is the appeal of plants. Behind their beauty and living greenery is a deep, underlying consciousness, a sense of universal spirituality of which their vitality is but the means of expression. Plants appeal to our senses, but this appeal goes deeper than the senses. We feel more in touch with the timeless sense of creation. The cosmic sense of plants goes beyond our senses, into our minds and our hearts, ineffably linking our nature with their own in one chain of life and consciousness—plant consciousness.

13

HIDDEN WISDOM

A strange and unexpected meeting ground has arisen between recent developments on the fringe of modern science and old folk tales about the trees. Both indicate that we live in a world in which plants are living, feeling, animate, and aware of fellow creatures. The wisdom of plants is reborn every day with each new green shoot coming up through the earth. This long-hidden wisdom has always been available for the asking. The people of old understood and lived with this wisdom. The key to our proper understanding of it begins in their tales, superstitions, and proverbs.

ANCIENT MIRRORS

Primitive man responded to the plants as beings with souls of their own and revered the energy within them as divine. Frazer, in *The Golden Bough*, pointed out that what we call "primitive man" is a simplistic catchall for a sophisticated sensibility that had highly evolved systems of rites and myths. Many of these belief systems centered on the worship of trees and still pertain today in many parts of the world. Such rites and myths provide us with an ancient mirror through which we can view our own nature.

BLOOD BROTHERS

African legends often relate that trees bleed, wail, cry, and suffer. Tribesmen feel that the trees are sensitive, and if they are to be cut down, the procedure must be gentle and sympathetic. One tribe of central Africa believes that if a tree is cut down, the angered spirit which inhabits it can cause the death of the chief and his family. After the first blow of the ax, the tribesman puts his mouth over the cut and sucks some of the sap, thus forming a "blood brotherhood" with the tree. After that he can cut down his blood brother at will.

HUNTIN

Along Africa's west coast people worshiped a god named Huntin, who lived in the giant silk-cotton trees. The tribesmen offered Huntin sacrifices of fowls and human beings. To cut down a tree animated by Huntin, a sacrifice of fowls and palm oil was offered. Omission of this sacrifice was punishable by death.

Some primitive tribes still talk to tree spirits. One tribe recites to the trees: "Be not uneasy, my friend, though we fell what we have been ordered to fell." Frazer points out that the spirits of vegetation are not always treated with the respect due a god. If they cannot be moved by honorable treatment, stronger measures are used. In one tribe the sorcerer strikes a blow with a hatchet to a barren tree, saying: "Will you now bear fruit or not? If you do not, I shall fell you." The reaction of the tree is heard through the mouth of another tribesman who has climbed another tree, "Yes, I will now bear fruit. I beg you not to fell me."

BETWEEN LIFE AND DEATH

What are the powers of these gods, these spirits of the trees? (1) The trees give rain and sunshine. Offerings in Burma were made to the spirit "nat" who controlled the rain from its home in a large tamarind tree. The people prayed: "O Lord 'nat,' have pity on us poor mortals, and stay not the rain. Inasmuch as our offering is given ungrudgingly, let the rain fall day and night." (2) The trees give life. A tribe in eastern Africa believes that every tree has a spirit and that its destruction is a matricide, as the tree provides the people with nourishment and life, as a mother does its child. (3) The trees are a bridge between life and death. An Australian tribe regards as sacred certain trees which are supposed to be transformations of their deceased fathers; hence they speak with reverence of these trees and are careful that they are not cut down or burned.

THE FRIGHTENED TREE

Tree myths pervaded the consciousness of ancient Europe. In a Cornish legend Tristan and Iseult were buried in the same church but at a distance from each other. Eventually ivy grew from each of their graves and met on the roof above. The oldest sanctuaries of the Germans were natural woods. The oak worship of the Druids was a familiar Celtic custom. Austrian peasants believed that trees feel cuts no less than a man feels his wounds, and they did not cut down a tree without asking permission. Until the fourteenth century, the Lithuanians believed in oracular oaks; breaking one of its twigs was a sin which could result in death or crippling. The Slavs performed a ritual on Christmas Eve in which an ax-man swung threateningly against a barren fruit tree, while another man stopped him, saying: "Do not cut it down; it will soon bear fruit." Three times the ax was swung and three times the second man interceded in the hope that the frightened tree would bear fruit in the next year.

IMITATIVE MAGIC

Legendary tales from Europe stem in part from the theory of imitative magic in which a person influences vegetation for good or evil according to the good or bad character of his acts or states. This principle was mutual: a plant could affect a man as much as a man could affect a plant. Frazer tells that in "Vedic times an application of this principle supplied a charm by which a banished prince might be restored to his kingdom. He had to eat food cooked on a fire which was fed with wood which had grown out of the stump of a tree which had been cut down. The recuperative power manifested by such a tree would in due course be communicated through the fire to the food, and so to the prince, who ate the food which was cooked on the fire which was fed with the wood which grew out of the tree."

A LIFE FOR A LIFE

We calmly shape, prune, and trim the plants with
which we live, thinking of them as decorative and
pleasing additions to our environments. We might
contemplate for a moment the intense role occupied
by the plants in ancient consciousness. Frazer reports
that the Germans punished those who peeled the bark
off a tree in the following way: "The culprit's navel
was to be cut out and nailed to the part of the tree
which he had peeled, and he was to be driven round
and round the tree, till all his guts were wound about
its trunk. The intention of the punishment clearly
was to replace the dead bark by a living substitute
taken from the culprit; it was a life for a life, the life
of a man for the life of a tree."

INDIAN SPIRITS

Much of the European pattern pertained in North America. The Hidetsa Indians believed that every natural object had a spirit, which was embodied in its shadow. They believed that the shade of the cottonwood possessed an intelligence which would aid them in their undertakings. The Iroquois believed that every form and species of plant life had its own spirit, and they honored these spirits by giving them thanks. In fact, in matters of life and death there is an interesting parallel between the consciousness of the Indians and the way in which we should perceive our plants. Plants ready to die act in a manner similar to that of the Indian. Nothing in particular may be wrong, but they choose to give up life. The only thing to do is to understand and show respect.

THE SUNFLOWER ROOT

Contemporary patterns of awareness and insight are very much inherent in the experiences of primitive Indians who gained mystic vision and spiritual knowledge through the ritualistic use of plants with hallucinogenic properties. Frazer reports that the Indians of British Columbia regarded the sunflower root as a mysterious being and observed certain taboos in connection with it. "Women who were engaged in digging or cooking the root must practice continence, and no man might come near the oven where the women were baking the root. When young people ate the first berries, roots, or other products of the season, they addressed a prayer to the sunflower root as follows: 'I inform thee that I intend to eat thee. Mayest thou always help me to ascend, so that I may always be able to reach the tops of mountains, and may I never be clumsy! I ask this from thee, Sunflower Root. Thou art the greatest of all in mystery.'"

AGREEMENT WITH THE LEAVES

Evidence of the heritage of old Indian plant-legends is to be found in the encounter of Mexican Indian sorcerer don Juan by Carlos Castaneda as described by the latter in *Journey to Ixtlan*. One day, while walking through the desert chapparral, don Juan gives him a lesson on plants. He tells him that plants are peculiar things, that they are alive and have feelings. At that point in the conversation a strong wind shook the leaves of nearby bushes. Don Juan uses this sign as an indication that he is in agreement with the leaves. During the walk, don Juan does not pick any plants, nor does he even show plants to his disciple. He walks along and lightly touches them as he passes by. Castaneda again informs him of his desire to learn about plants, peyote in particular. The master agrees to tell him everything he knows about them and how this knowledge can be used. This delights Castaneda, but in don Juan's world, reality (particularly when involved with plants) is no simple matter. As he says in a final remark; "Perhaps there is nothing to learn about plants, because there is nothing to say about them."

FOREST GOD

In primitive belief systems the plant was thought to be the actual spiritual entity. The next step, which is actually a more recent interpretation of earlier legends, recognized the plant or tree as a home in which the gods resided and which they could leave at their wish. Frazer pointed out that it was a case of "animism passing into polytheism. Instead of regarding each tree as a living and conscious being, man now sees in it merely a lifeless, inert mass, tenanted for a longer or shorter time by a supernatural being who, as he can pass freely from tree to tree, thereby enjoys a certain right of possession of Lordship over the trees, and, ceasing to be a tree soul, becomes a forest god." The tree spirit had been divorced from particular trees. The next step, the role of the Greeks, was to present these forest gods in human form.

THE LINGERING GODS

The Greeks were not prepared to change irrevocably the plant gods and tree spirits into humanized form. The older images continued to find a relevant place midst their newly evolved mythology. Syrinx, fleeing from Pan, was changed by her father Lodon into a reed. The three daughters of Suna and Clymere, mourning after Zeus hurled their presumptuous brother into the river Eridamus, were changed into poplars and grew by the riverside. Phyllis, who hanged herself because she thought her lover Demophon had deserted her, was changed into an almond tree; when her repentant lover embraced it, its branches broke into leaf and flower. The tree gods lingered on.

THE ORACULAR OAK OF ZEUS

The ancient Greeks believed that the actual seat of Zeus was in the Oak of Zeus at Dodana. This most venerable tree in the grove of oaks was believed to be an oracle whose answers were given by the murmur of the spring that flowed from among its roots, or by lots drawn from an urn placed beneath.

THE SACRED LAUREL

The Greeks believed that god-like spirits dwelled within the trees. They also believed that human beings could be changed into trees. In Ovid's *Metamorphosis*, Daphne, fleeing from Apollo, prayed to her mother Earth to deliver her, whereupon the ground opened and rescued her. In her place sprang up a laurel tree. Apollo, coming upon the laurel, declared that it would be sacred to him forever.

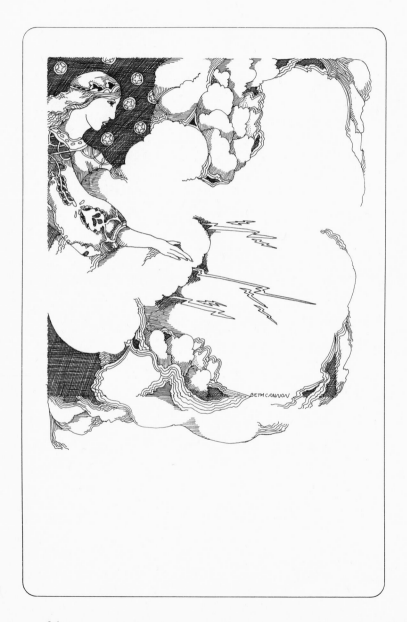

SPIRITUAL DESCENDANTS

The Greeks filled the cosmic universe with gods in human form and clothing, but these beings were merely a new image for the wielding of the powers invested in the older tree gods. Still later, following the Greeks, such powers would be incarnated in the flesh and blood of actual human beings, direct descendants of the spirits of the trees.

THE SACRED FIG TREE

The ancient Romans worshiped tree spirits, such as the sacred fig tree of Romulus. Another holy tree, growing outside the center of the city, was looked after by the entire community. Its physical condition was the cause of city-wide comment and concern. Whenever it appeared to be withering, crowds would appear from throughout the city with buckets of water and gather in a symbolic mass gesture of concern.

WAR GOD AND VEGETATION GOD

Worship of vegetation gods is at the base of the structure of many ancient faiths which today find expression in modern religions. The inception of the Judaic-Christian heritage was the creation of Yahweh as an alternative to worship of the vegetation gods. The Hebrews were a nomadic tribe, dependent on animals, not land, for their sustenance. Yahweh was a tribal god and war god. People who depended on crops worshiped Baal, the god of land fertility, who was symbolized in either animal or vegetable form. When times were peaceful, and people turned their attention to the land, Baal was the primary god. During times of war the people felt a need to worship a war god, and thus they turned to Yahweh.

CAIN AND ABEL

We sit in our devegetated cities of cement and wonder how the world might differ had the vegetation gods prevailed over the Jewish war god. Such was not the case, however. The battle of the ancient gods is illustrated by the biblical story of Cain and Abel. Cain presented a vegetation offering to Yahweh; his offer was refused. Abel offered a slaughtered animal; his offer was accepted.

The heritage of the vegetation gods is evident in the many references to trees and posts appearing in the Old Testament in connection with divine appearances. Jehovah appeared to Abraham beneath the oak tree in Mamre, and to Moses in the burning bush. At Shechan, Joshua "took a great stone, and sat it up under an oak that was by the sanctuary of the Lord." Deborah the prophetess "dwelt under the plum tree of Deborah, between Rona and Bethel in Mount Ephriam; and the Children of Israel came up to her for judgment." It was "under an oak which was in Ophrah" that the Angel of the Lord came and spoke to Gideon, telling him that it was he who was to save Israel from the hand of the Midinites.

DAVID IN THE MULBERRY TREES

In biblical narratives trees no longer appear as gods but as oracles, as mediums of communication between gods and men. David, upon asking the Lord how and when he should attack the Philistines, was told, "Thou shalt not go up; but fetch a compass behind them, and come upon them even against the mulberry trees, that thou shalt bestir thyself, for then shall the Lord go out before thee, to smite the host of the Philistines."

"O ABSALOM, MY SON, MY SON!"

The oracular trees of the old testament played an active part in the implementation of God's will. King David's reign was threatened by a revolt led by his son Absalom. David asked his lieutenants to deal gently with him. A great battle ensued. "The people went out into the field against Israel; and the battle was in the forest of Ephraim. And the people of Israel were smitten there before the servants of David, and there was a great slaughter there that day of twenty thousand men. For the battle was there spread over the face of all the country; and the forest devoured more people that day than the sword devoured. And Absalom chanced to meet the servants of David. And Absalom was riding upon his mule, and the mule went under the thick boughs of a great terebinth, and he was taken up between the heaven and the earth; and the mule that was under him went on." Absalom, hanging from the terebinth by his beautiful long hair, was slain by Joab. Upon hearing the news, David wept; "and as he went, thus he said: 'O my son Absalom, my son, my son Absalom! would I had died for thee, O Absalom, my son, my son!' "

ISAIAH AND THE CARPENTER

The people who worshiped the Jewish God Yahweh learned to believe in a universal spirit living and working in all things. Thus Isaiah inveighed against a carpenter of more primitive beliefs: "He hameth him down cedars, and taketh the cypress and the oak, which he strengtheneth for himself among the trees of the forest: he planteth an ash, and the rain doth nourish it. Then shall it be for a man to burn: for he will take there of, and warm himself; yea he kindleth it and baketh bread; yea he maketh a god and worshipeth it; he maketh a graven image and falleth down thereto. He burneth part thereof in the fire; with part thereof he eateth flesh; he roasteth meat, and is satisfied; yea, he warmeth himself and saith: "Aha, I am warm, I have seen the fire: and the residue thereof he maketh a god, even his graven image; he falleth down to unto it, and saith, Deliver me, for thou art my God."

SPIRITS INNUMERABLE

Isaiah's belief in a single universal being is indicative of a great leap in man's symbol-making capability. And yet there were still many around him who believed not that the trees necessarily were their gods, but that there were innumerable spirits which could find a home in all things. In principle, a single universal being would have the property of being in all things; yet in practice, this being was construed in the image of man. Spiritual reality centered in a god who now resembled and indeed acted like a man and bore no resemblance to the trees and plants in which he found his original home.

No one knows the time of year that Jesus was born. The selection of the Christmas date to celebrate his birth was an attempt by the church to co-opt and supersede the ancient primitive festival of the winter solstice, a pre-Christian rejoicing that the year had turned and the sun would soon rise in the sky and bring forth the spring. The celebration of May Day was originally a serious pagan religious observance paying homage to the spirits in the trees. The dance around the maypole was a religious ritual. The spirit of the tree lived also in the symbolic maypole taken from the tree. The May Queen was, in origin, a human form of the tree spirit.

47

"BEHOLD THE MESSIAH"

The humanization of the universal spirit in the being of Jesus was a difficult and unwarranted adjustment for his fellow Jews. One famous rabbi used to say: "If there be a plant in your hand when they say to you: 'Behold the Messiah!' . . . go and plant the plant, and afterward go out and greet him."

TREE OF LIFE

Christian reverence for trees bears the heritage of Greek mythology, in which the trees were considered to be animate beings with god-like powers. Those powers produced rain and sunshine. They were responsible for the well-being of crops and livestock. They caused the fruitfulness and multiplication of the human population. To this population they have appeared and been known under such names as Zeus, Pan, Yahweh, and Christ. But as the primitive chief said to the Christian missionary when questioned on his view of God: "We know that at night someone goes by amongst the trees, but we never speak of it." Even in the time of Jesus, the tree remained sacred, as witnessed by John's comments on God in the New Testament: "And he showed me a pure river of life, clear as the crystal, proceeding out of the throne of God and of the Lamb. In the midst of the street of it, and on either side of the river, was the tree of life, which bore twelve manner of fruits, and yielded her fruit every month: and the leaves of the tree were for the healing of the nations."

THE SKY ABOVE

And so the heavens, the mystical place of spirituality, passed from the tree tops to the sky above. And the race of mankind passes through the same experience:

I remember, I remember
  The fir trees dark and high
I used to think their slender tips
  were close against the sky,
It was a childish ignorance
  But now 'tis little joy
To know I'm farther off from Heav'n
  Then when I was a boy.

TOM HOOD

THE SAME PLANT

We, the modern children of Ask and Embla, are among the most recent creatures to evolve. We come upon the earth and find what has already existed. We create nothing ourselves, nothing but names. We have not been separated from nature, for nature is but one of the names we have invented, a category which fixes our world in a particular compartment. Instead of a spiritual wholeness, there is man and a nature which is outside man—a dumb, inert nature to be used, manipulated, and modified. In this nature the names we give to orders and varieties of plants deceive us into creating imaginary types which we believe to be fixed, whereas they are probably representatives of the same plant, which continues to modify its organs slowly in accordance with circumstances, too slowly and too anciently to be visible to the newly focused eye of man. The plant came upon the earth before man.

LINNEAUS

How did these remarkably spiritual plants and trees become known as mere objects? The narrowness of vision began with the science of Aristotle and culminated in the nineteenth-century work of Linneaus, the great botanist who developed a system of classification and categories which created a dead scheme of life out of the living world of plants and trees. The rigid scientific dogma of Linneaus turned our perception of the lovely spiritual beings of our past into inert objects, labeled and grouped under ponderous Latin names. His categories became walls between ourselves and our past; his classifications are an impenetrable barrier behind which stands the spiritual heritage of the plants. What was once natural became "nature," a separation, an unnatural consciousness.

THE SOUL OF PLANTS

Not all the voices of science echo the teachings of Linneaus. Gustav Fechner, a nineteenth-century scientist, attempted to re-create a wholeness of vision. The science of that day believed that plants, in all events, were lower than humans and that all that could be claimed for plants was a faint echo of human feeling. But Fechner said that plants "have even a keener and richer responsibility than animals. In fact, I do believe the plant is higher than we are, only in a lower realm. Precisely because it lacks a higher life of soul, the life of sense impression, though it is a lower stage, may in that state reach a degree of development which in us is lacking." His book was entitled *The Soul of Plants*.

DEEPLY ROOTED, DEEPLY EXPERIENCED

In the age of nineteenth-century materialism Fechner's realization that plants have souls was readily dismissed by the shamans of the scientific community. Fechner answered their arguments in part by pointing out that "the oak could easily retort against us all the arguments we use against her soul. How freshly she puts forth branches on all sides, brings forth leaf after leaf, and adorns herself anew with what she herself generates. We put on only outward adornments which we have not generated, and must leave our body as it was given once and for all. Man and animals run around, distract themselves with pleasures, touch and experience things which are apart. But devotion to home is also advantageous. There are many very quiet and sedentary types of endeavor which need to be thoroughly lived through and deeply experienced. Animals run superficially over places where the plant is deeply rooted, the animal breaks through the radius of the circle the plant fills completely."

RESEMBLANCES

Fechner speculated on the possibility that plants have souls; and Charles Darwin considered the possibility that plants have the ability to think. In his study *The Power of Movement in Plants,* he observed that it was "impossible not to be struck with the resemblance between the foregoing movements of plants and many of the actions performed unconsciously by the lower animals. With plants an astonishingly small stimulus suffices, and even with allied plants one may be highly sensitive to the slightest continued pressure, and another highly sensitive to a slight momentary touch. The habit of moving at certain periods is inherited both by plants and animals; and several other points of similitude have been specified. But the most striking resemblance is the localization of their sensitiveness, and the transmission of an influence from the excited part to another which consequently moves. Yet plants do not of course possess nerves or a central nervous system; and we may infer that with animals such structures seem only for the more perfect transmission of impressions, and for the more complete intercommunication of several parts."

TRANSFORMATIONS

Whether plants have souls or not, one thing is evident: plants bridge the nether world between life and death. Plants make beautiful, colorful, and life-sustaining forms from earth, water, air, and other substances, a creation of life from inorganic matter. We humans sustain our lives through the consumption of living, organic matter in the form of plants or fellow animals. Where we only transform living matter, the plants create and bring life to the world.

MOVEMENTS IN PLANTS

Although Darwin did not postulate a nervous system in plants, he did state unequivocally that the part of the plant that develops into the primary root acts in a similar manner to the brain of lower animals. "We believe that there is no structure in plants more wonderful, as far as its functions are concerned, than the tip of the radicle. If the tip be lightly burnt or cut, it transmits an influence to the upper adjoining part, causing it to bend away from the affected side; and, what is more surprising, the tip can distinguish between a slightly harder and softer object, by which it is simultaneously pressed on opposite sides. If however, the radicle is pressed by a similar object a little above the top, the pressed part does not transmit any influence to the more distant parts, but bends abruptly toward the object."

PLANT BRAIN

Darwin observed a parallel between plant movement and the brain in lower animals. "In almost every case we can clearly perceive the final purpose or advantage of the several movements. Two, or perhaps more, of the exciting courses often simultaneously act on the tip, and one conquers the other, no doubt in accordance with its importance for the life of the plant. The course pursued by the radicle in penetrating the ground must be determined by the tip; hence it has acquired such diverse kinds of sensitiveness. It is hardly an exaggeration to say that the tip of the radicle, thus endowed, and having the adjoining parts, acts like the brain of one of the lower animals; the brain being seated within the anterior end of the body, receiving impressions from the sense organs, and directing the several movements."

THE SPINELESS CACTI

Luther Burbank developed over 2,000 distinct species of plants, more new forms of plant life than any other man. Part of his work was the demonstration that plants adapt themselves to human wishes. During his experiments, he built mental pictures of new plants and proceeded to create through breeding the exact plant formed in his mind. An example of this procedure is the spineless cactus. He noticed that cacti growing in the desert had defensive characteristics, such as spines and poisons, suited to a long past era when self-defense was necessary against predator animals. Burbank believed that a climate of love was necessary for the evolution of a new spineless variety. He talked to his plants, saying, "You have nothing to fear. You don't need your defensive thorns. I will protect you." His method was successful; he developed a thornless variety of cactus.

ONE VAST PLANT

The science of Burbank was a strange and effective blend of pure experimentation, love, and a universal cosmology: "My theory of the laws and underlying principles of plant creation is, in many respects, opposed to the theories of the materialists. I am a sincere believer in a higher power than man's. All my investigations have led me away from the idea of a dead material universe tossed about by various forces, to that of a universe which is absolutely all force, life, soul, thought, or whatever we may choose to call it. Every atom, molecule, plant, animal, or planet, is only an aggregation of organized unit forces, held in place by stronger forces, thus holding them for a time latent, though teeming with inconceivable power. All life on our planet is, so to speak, just on the outer fringe of this infinite ocean of force. The universe is not half dead, but all alive." An alive universe, a vibrant, vital reality. And where is man, the center, the sense of the humanistic universe? Burbank stated: "I now see humanity as one vast plant, needing for its highest fulfillment only love, and intelligent crossing, and selection."

THE VANISHING BOUNDARY LINE

Some years after the observations of Darwin and Burbank, the noted Indian scientist Sir Jagadis Chandra Bose began to study plants through merging the empirical Western procedures with the introspection of his Eastern heritage. Through this approach he believed he was able to break through the silences of long uncommunicative natural realms. Bose invented the crescograph, a valuable device which measures electrical potential. His investigations led him to and through the farthest edge of the physics and physiology of his day. "To my amazement," he stated, "I found boundary lines vanishing, and points of contact emerging, between the realms of the living and the nonliving. Inorganic matter was perceived as anything but inert. It was a thrill under the action of multitudinous forces."

A SENSITIVE NERVOUS SYSTEM

Do plants have a nervous system? Darwin believed that in a limited way plants had an ability to "think," and possessed properties similar in nature to the brain of a lower animal. But he did not go so far as to postulate the existence of a nervous system in plants. Yet the evolution of the technology available for the study of plants, in this case Bose's crescograph, created a need for a reevaluation of this question. Bose was convinced that, beyond any doubt, plants had a nervous system similar to that of humans. "The telltale charts of my crescograph," he said, "are evidence for the most skeptical that plants have a sensitive nervous system and a varied emotional life. Love, hate, joy, fear, pleasure, pain, excitability, stupor, and countless other appropriate responses to stimuli are as universal in plants as in animals."

THE SCIENTIST AND THE SWAMI

In his book *Autobiography of a Yogi*, Swami Yoga-
nanda captures the import of Bose's work. He recounts
an interview with Bose: "'I [Bose] will attach the
crescograph to this fern; the magnification is tremen-
dous. If a snail crawl were enlarged in the same proportion, the creature would appear to be traveling
like an express train!' My gaze was fixed eagerly on
the screen which reflected the magnified fern shadow.
Minute life movements were now clearly perceptible.
The plant was growing before my fascinated eyes.
The scientist touched the tip of the fern with a small
metal bar. The developing pantomime came to an
abrupt halt, resuming its eloquent rhythms as the rod
was withdrawn. . . .' You saw how any slight outside interference is detrimental to the sensitive tissues.
Watch I will now administer chloroform, and then
give an antidote'. . . . The effect of chloroform dis-
continued all growth; the antidote was revivifying.
The evolutionary gestures of the green held me more
raptly than a movie plot."

THE CHLOROFORMED TREE

Bose presented a model of a sophisticated nervous system in plants by which they transform sensations into motor impulses. He showed that stimulants and depressants such as alcohol, chloroform, and caffeine affected plants the same way as they affect humans. In one famous experiment, a giant tree was chloroformed and then successfully transplanted, an operation which previously had been impossible. Given caffein, his plants became agitated. Given alcohol, they swayed and acted in such a manner that Bose considered them drunk.

PLANT FEELINGS

Bose was the first scientist to show experimentally the existence of feelings in plants. He proved that plant cells open to one another and are in communication. Because of his work, we now know that plants do feel, even if we don't know how they do it. Feeling and sensitivity were the subject of many of Bose's experiments. According to Fechner's translator: "In one of these the apparatus he devised enabled the audience to see how a turnip shuddered on one side when the other side was pricked. This proves not only a sensation but the transmission of it. The so-called sensitive plant (mimosa sensitiva) has no nerves, and yet one can plainly see that when one leaf is touched, the sensation, or an awareness of it, is transmitted at a certain rate of speed to a distance relatively great along the twigs and branches. This is not a solitary instance of a plant which is visibly sensitive. Venus's-flytrap has a more obvious reason for making a brisker movement when it is touched. Most plants, having no reason to make a movement in response to such a stimulus, give no visible evidence of sensitivity—and yet they may be as sensitive as the mimosa."

HELP FROM THE PLANTS

Bose's work with plants gave rise to new possibilities for studying the electrical waves that exist and control the intelligence of both plants and men. In 1938 *The New York Times* reported: "It was determined that when nerves transmit messages between the brain and other parts of the body, tiny electrical impulses are being generated. These impulses have been measured by delicate galvanometers and magnified millions of times by modern amplifying apparatus. Until now, no satisfactory method had been found to study the passage of the impulses along the nerve fibers in living animals or man because of the great speed with which these impulses travel. . . . Electrical nerve impulses in the plant were found to be much slower than those in animals. Certain long single cells of plants are virtually identical with those of single nerve fibers in animals. The cells of the nitelle propagate electrical waves that are similar in every way, except velocity, to those of the nerve fibers in minerals and men. This discovery allowed taking slow-motion pictures of the passage of the electrical impulses in nerves. . . . The nitelle plant may thus become a sort of Rosetta stone for deciphering the closely guarded secrets close to the very borderland of mind and matter."

MUTUAL SENSES

From Fechner we have a "soul" of plants; from Darwin, a plant brain; from Bose, a nervous system and a pattern of feelings. But plants can also see, and hear, and smell, touch, and taste. Most interesting of all, they seem to possess some strange psychic sense of communication between both themselves and other living matter—some sixth sense, a plant sense, a plant consciousness. In *The Human Side of Plants*, Dixon notes many mutual senses between plants and humans. For example, plants are sensitive to the presence or absence of light. They approach a sunny spot from the shade, or a shady spot from the sun. An approaching shadow will cause some plants to close their petals.

THE VISION OF PLANTS

Plants have vision, or rather they are as sensitive to light in their own way as we are in ours. Whereas our light sensitivity is located in our eyes, light is enjoyed very differently by the plants, whose entire life culminates in light. Fechner pointed out that "the plant, to be sure, has no eye like ours, nor any contrivance for forming a picture of an object. But what use would this be to it? It does not have to run around to the object nor to stretch out for it. To this end we have to be guided by a picture. To the plant everything it needs comes of itself. For the same reason the plant probably is deaf to every sound; for words make no sense to it, and the warning of an inarticulate noise would be of no use to it so long as it is unable to budge from the spot."

VIBRATIONS

But plants do hear. There are instances of sensitive plants that are susceptible to every vibration, for sound is the effect of vibrations. Recent experiments conducted by Dorothy Rettallack indicate that music affects the growth rate and well-being of plants. The basic experiment was to subject two similar groups of plants in separate compartments to different kinds of music through high fidelity speakers. The plants in the first room listened to cacophonous rock and roll. They cringed and died. They leaned away from the music, and even their roots began to grow the other way. The plants in the second compartment listened to soft classical music. They flourished and grew healthier every day. The leaves of one plant actually reached out and wrapped themselves around the loudspeaker.

HUMAN POWERS OF PLANTS

Plants have a sense of touch. The action of the tentacles of the sundew, when touched by a foreign substance, is evidence of this ability to feel. Plant consciousness of heat and cold frequently has been proved by approaching a flower with a hot iron; there may be no change in the light, but with a change in temperature, the flower closes, as if to protect its precious children from harm. Plants can smell. An odor offensive to a plant will cause it to close and, if endured long, will kill it. The wonderful power of plants to detect approaching rain, or the nearness of water, may be attributed to a sense of smell. Plants can taste. The taste of some plants for salt, and of others for sugar, iron, zinc, or other substances is very marked. There can be little question that the prevalence or scarcity of a favorite food has much to do with the habitat of a plant.

PLANT ACTION

The presence of both special psychic and physical senses in plants is noted by Dixon. He believes that in addition to seeing, hearing, touching, tasting, and smelling, plants also exhibit psychic tendencies. For instance, a plant is able to discover objects necessary to its welfare, an example of which is to be found wherever climbing or creeping plants grow. The support is invisible from the plant's starting point, and there is no odor which might indicate direction. The only explanation is a psychic sense. The special physical sense of plants is evident in the fact that our house plants, which in their domestication have assumed more or less artificial forms, will, on being returned to their natural habitats, reassume their natural forms.

SPIRITUAL HERITAGE

We have seen that primitive man lived in an intense spiritual relationship with the plant life that was his environment and sustenance. The Druids, the Hebrews, the Greeks, the Romans, and the Christians built religious systems that were based on the foundations of plant worship. With the coming of Jesus, the spirit of the trees underwent a final humanization and became construed in the image of a single human entity, be it Christ, the man-like Jewish god, or even a universal spirit, a spirit conceived as being alive in all things but seen by man as a mirror of his own humanity. These developments, and the rise of scientism during the Middle Ages, totally despiritualized the plants, leaving them inert, dumb objects. The plants, however, have not changed. It is we who are different. The plants have lost nothing. We have lost everything. We have lost our spiritual heritage.

BETH CANNON

79

NEW QUESTIONS

Modern experiences and events have forced us to reappraise our relationship to plants and raise our consciousness to find a conceptual level broad enough to understand just what they are and who we are. The experiments of Fechner, Darwin, Burbank, and Bose raised more questions than they answered. In recent years further evidence has called for a reexamination of the bridge between the scientific and the spiritual worlds. Whereas previous questions centered on plant sensations, the new plant consciousness dwells on plant action: the intelligence, emotions, and spirituality of plants.

OCCULT, EXTRASENSORY,
OR JUST PLAIN MAGIC

During the 1950s, Franklin Loehr, a Protestant minister, attempted to establish what Burbank had suggested—that the power of the human mind could cause plants to react in a certain manner. Reverend Loehr believed that prayer was such an objective power and that it was capable of making a visible, meaningful, and repeatable difference in plant growth. According to Loehr, "Powers hitherto considered occult, extrasensory, or just plain magic were given scientific proof by the three-year laboratory research here related. Man *does* have spiritual powers beyond his physical being." Had he not been reared in and educated by the Christian faith, perhaps he might have said that "the plants have spiritual powers beyond their physical being."

PRAYED-OVER PLANTS

Loehr's experiment went as follows: "Two sealed jars of water were purchased from a nearby grocery store. One was put away. The other was brought up to a prayer circle. First, group prayer was given to this jar of water, then it was passed from hand to hand, so that each member of the prayer circle could give it personal prayer. Then we gave it a closing group prayer—perhaps twenty to thirty minutes in all. Next, three sets of twin pans were put out. Eight kernels of corn went into each pan in the first set. The next set received eight lima beans each. In the final set, sweet pea pods were used. In one pan of each set the prayed-over water was poured, in the other, the ordinary water." This is Loehr's basic experiment, and the results, though varying in specific cases, show a marked trend. "Over the years a general proportion has held throughout: two out of three prayed-for plants came out ahead." Loehr commented that "science is simply the research method for getting the facts in any field. The material realm is the easiest part. The bringing of science to a spiritual realm is harder."

A 42-POUND CABBAGE

Another recent example of "God-centered" plant care is the work of a plant-growing community of 140 people in Findhorn Bay, Scotland. The group is lead by Peter Caddy, whose wife Elixir makes a daily contact "at the highest spiritual level which brings specific instructions dealing with plant care." According to one eyewitness, the Caddy's and their group live in a wonderland of vegetation: "Fruits and trees of all sorts were in blossom—in short, one of the most vigorous and productive of small gardens I have ever seen, with a quality of taste and color unsurpassed. Many species of broad-leaved trees and shrubs were thriving, yet the caravan site is on the landward slope of windswept dunes. The soil is simply sand and gravel on which grows spiky grass. Other folks on the site, seeing the lovely burgeoning around their neighbor's caravans, put in cabbages and daffodils which came up as miserable specimens. Caddy claims to have grown a 42-pound cabbage!"

THE DEVAS

The Findhorn group has created their own updated form of plant worship. Their invocation is to the world of the "Devas," those netherworld spirits who have been described as the architects of plant forms and the elemental beings of nature who are the craftsmen carrying out the divine laws of plant growth and form. The group considers their spiritual work to be a cooperative effort between three kingdoms: man, that of the Devas, and that of the nature spirits. "The Devas are the Angelic Beings who wield the archetypal forces. There is one of these for every species in the plant kingdom. The Devas deal with forces and with pattern or form. The Nature Spirits, or Elementals, are concerned with using energy to build form, e.g., causing the sap to rise. In effect, the Devas provide the blueprint and energy and the Nature Spirits carry out the actual work."

ATROPHIED SENSIBILITY

Whether we believe in Devas or not, the fact is that the Findhorn group has transformed a desert into a beautiful, bountiful, and unexplainable garden. Their primitive ancestors, to whom the nature spirits were immediately visible and directly experienced, would find nothing strange in their approach to plants. Their explanation is that "with the development of modern intellectual consciousness this knowledge has dropped out of our thinking and is often written off as so much superstition. An alternative explanation is that the organs of perception of the supersensible world would have atrophied in modern man as part of the price to be paid for the evolving of an analytical scientific mind. The nature spirits may be just as real as they ever were, though not to be perceived except by those who can redevelop the faculty to see and experience them. Modern spiritual science shows that this is possible and that the conscious investigation of higher worlds is of utmost importance in our understanding of life."

WE LISTEN

Through their love and devotion, the Findhorn gardeners work unconsciously with the spirits of the plants. Their attempt at direct mental contact with such forces is not a new development in our relationship with natural forces, but a return to an ancient ritual. Their invocation of these spirits is direct and simple:

"1 We acknowledge they exist and offer our love and thanks.

2 We invoke their aid in inner thought contact.

3 We listen, with alert attention (whether or not we can consciously receive an answer).

4 Again we *give thanks* with love from the heart."

SCIENTIFIC TWILIGHT

"We're getting into another dimension, a scientific twilight area in which something can go from point to point without going between them and without consuming time to get there . . . but that won't be as wierd as we might think; it could simply mean that some of the things that were once laughed at in theoretical physics are finally falling into place." These are the words of Cleve Backster, a lie detector expert who once did work for the CIA. Backster's work with plant feelings, emotions, and perceptions has aroused considerable curiosity and interest. The questions raised by his research threaten the foundations of our modern sensory world and seem to thrust us back to the time of a more intimate and immediate relationship between plants and man.

THREATENED PLANT

To relate the importance of Backster's work, it is necessary to explore his basic experiments. One day, while attempting to measure the rate at which water rose in a plant root, Backster happened upon an unexplainable phenomenon. Placing an electrode on a philodendron plant, he hooked the plant up to a lie detector (polygraph) and attempted to apply the threat-to-well-being principle which is used on human subjects. "I first tried to arouse the plant by immersing a plant leaf in a cup of hot coffee. But there was no measurable reaction. After a nine-minute interim, I decided to obtain a match and burn the plant leaf being tested. At the instant of the decision, at 13 minutes 55 seconds of chart time, there was a dramatic change in the PGR tracing pattern in the form of an abrupt and prolonged upward sweep of the recording pen. I had not moved, or touched, the plant, so the timing of the PGR pen activity suggested to me that the tracing might have been triggered by the mere thought of the harm I intended to inflict upon the plant. This occurrence, if repeatable, would tend to indicate the possible existence of some undefined perception in the plant."

PLANT PERCEPTIONS

Backster's experiments continued. One of six students was chosen by lot to destroy a plant. Keeping his identity secret from Backster, the student killed the plant. The only witness was a second plant. This plant was then hooked up to a polygraph and each of the six students was taken to the plant. The only noticeable reaction registered by the plant was when the plant killer walked by. In another experiment, three plants were placed in separate rooms and attached to polygraphs. Several doors away an automatic device periodically dumped live brine shrimp into boiling water, killing them instantly. At the *exact* moment that the shrimp hit the water and died, the three plants registered reactions on the polygraph similar to that of severe emotional stress in humans.

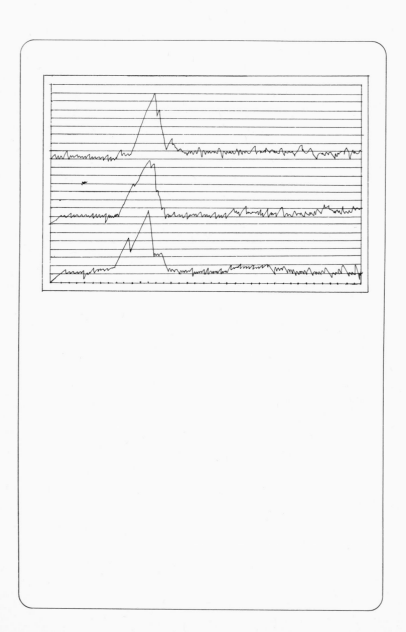

STRANGE SIGNALS

What are the plants saying to us? Backster's work indicates several possibilities:

1 Plants have emotions and feel apprehension, fear, pleasure, and relief.

2 Plants react to threats against their well-being.

3 Plants have the ability to think.

4 Plants react to the death of living things in their vicinity.

5 Plants know the private thoughts of their caretakers and respond to situations affecting these people.

6 When any cell life dies, it broadcasts a signal to other living cells.

7 The signal broadcast by plants is a strange signal of perception that is beyond our current scientific mode of explanation. It can only be explained as a nontime-consuming form of communication outside the electromagnetic spectrum. Thus, according to scientific principle, it does not exist. Yet Backster claims his evidence indicates otherwise.

8 Total memory may not be located in the brain, or in the central nervous system, but perhaps goes down to the single-cell level. This pertains to both plants and humans. Thus, according to Backster, the human "brain may be just a switching mechanism, and not necessarily the memory storage organ we've thought it to be."

PRIMARY PERCEPTION

What Backster calls "primary perception" in plants is the ability of individual cells to communicate to each other with signals that are nontime-consuming. In other words, Backster's "primary perception" is a euphemism for "extrasensory perception." Only Backster feels that there is nothing magical about it. He believes that the questions raised by his work will in time be answered by physicists who he hopes will become interested in his experiments. In the meantime, the scientific community has yet to duplicate his findings, and until they do, he will remain a hero in the occult world of unexplainable realities. Concerning the strange signals of awareness, Backster points out that it is only possible to describe what they are not. They do not exist within known frequencies, and distance and space do not seem to affect them. Experiments that traverse hundreds of miles demonstrate no change in the effect of the plant signals. Backster uses as his reality base the evidence of nontime-consuming communication known in Eastern religions, that is, a universe in total balance, a oneness of all things. The questions raised by his work cannot as yet be answered. Backster admits that he does not know what kind of energy wave may carry the thoughts, feelings, and emotions of a human to a plant. It's another dimension, a scientific twilight.

THE UNEXPLAINABLE

Backster's work should not be dismissed as "occult" or "supernatural" merely because it has no scientific explanation. In fact, what our modern, civilized, and sophisticated minds find unexplainable (and to some, therefore, unacceptable), our earliest ancestors, dwelling among the plant spirits, would find visible and obvious. The limitations of our scientific explanations are self-imposed. We have created a construct of a sensory and perceptual world in which certain rules apply. Backster raises the possibility that reality may not conveniently fit into such a frame. Our entire scientific framework is based on the cumulative wealth of human experience. There seem to be entire areas of primitive knowledge that early scientists chose to overlook or reject. To reach back and accept the ancient divinity and wisdom of plants is to balance the arbitrariness of our own concepts, useful as they are in their applications in other spheres.

PRAYER TO WHOM? TO WHAT?

Speculation as to a possible mechanism for Backster's phenomenon centers on the theory of a release of quantum energy by a human during a certain state, which the plant picks up and converts into an enzymatic reaction. Such an enzymatic reaction changes the plant's potential electrical discharge, which is what Backster picks up on his polygraph. One of the reasons postulated for the effectiveness of plants in measuring the emotions of humans is that both men and plants have weak electrical fields, and therefore human penetration of the plant's electrical field will result in a significant response. Backster believes that if we think negatively about one plant and positively about another, the first, can be made to die, and the second, to grow into a healthy state. He points out that plants appreciate being watered, worry when approached by a sniffing dog, actually "faint" when violence threatens their well-being, and are sympathetic to any danger posed to neighboring animals, insects, or plants. Backster is beginning to enlarge the scope of his thinking to include more than science. "I'm beginning to see a lot of similarity between the vehicle involved here and the phenomenon of prayer. As a former agnostic who didn't take the trouble to be an atheist, I see some very high-level theological and spiritual implications of all this—it opens the way for scientific exploration of the concept and seems to indicate a scientific justification for the power of prayer." But prayer to whom? To what?

TOO DEEP FOR TEARS

Backster's work has awakened in us a fellowship with plants and trees. This companionship, especially for those of us living in concrete and cement cities, has too long been dormant. Few plants and trees exist near us. In light of today's environmental conditions, they can be anything but healthy. Their spirits, if existing, must be sad—a sadness too deep for tears. We do not necessarily have to ascribe divine or even friendly spirits and watchful gods to our plants and trees, but we must begin to endow these forms of life with the mystery and wonder which they offered their human neighbors of old. From the earliest history to the present day there have been races and individuals who believe in the spirituality of plants. In recent centuries the assertion that plants have a sense of spirituality, souls, and intelligence has been held up to ridicule. Yet the pervasiveness and tenacity of plant spirituality over the ages causes us to pause and ponder. Perhaps the plants will give us no answers to the questions we ask about the life in their cells. But who can give the answer? We can guess at it as we work among them, changing, shaping, and modifying their lives. The whole answer is not always ours to give.

POWER & WISDOM

The plants, once the spiritual center of our universe, also give us the power to radically alter our perceptions of ourselves, of them, and of the world. In *The Teachings of Don Juan*, Castaneda recounts his experiences with his Mexican brujos. Don Juan introduces his disciple to three hallucinogenic plants long known amongst the North American Indians for their ancient, magical, curative, and ecstatic powers. As a modern-day witch doctor, don Juan teaches Castaneda how to use the plants: peyote (*lophophora williamsii*) to acquire wisdom, or insight in the proper way to conduct his life; and jimson weed (*Datura inoxia syn. D. Meteloides*) and a mushroom (*Psilicybe Mexican*) to acquire power, or what don Juan calls an "ally."

MESCALITO

Don Juan envisions the powers of plants incarnate in a humanized form. Mescalito is anthropomorphized as a male, due to his qualities of being a protector and a teacher. Don Juan explains that mescalito takes you to another world, not heaven, but through heaven to another realm of being. Mescalito is not God, or one of the gods, but merely a protector, a teacher, or in don Juan's term "a power." This power is not ourselves, but exists outside us. Yet he appears in a different form to everyone who invokes his magic.

THE DATURA PLANT

Don Juan presented Castaneda with a *Datura* plant. After receiving the plant, he transplanted the root, which in a year grew into a large bush. After the seeds appeared, and the seedpods dried, don Juan felt the time was right for a lesson on the "devil's weed." This lesson concerned mastering the use of the second portion of the root, which he considered a primary step in learning. This part of the root allows one to instantaneously traverse time and space, or in don Juan's terminology, "to see." Seeing enables one to "fly through the air to see what is going on at any place he chooses." Don Juan's use of this phrase is literal: he really means what he says and points out that the power of "devil's weed" is such that one who masters the second portion can do things that are unimaginable to us when in ordinary states of consciousness. When Castaneda asks "What kind of things, don Juan?" the reply is "I can't tell you that. Every man is different."

CANNABIS INDICA

The impact of the lessons of don Juan—the general wisdom and plant consciousness of the American and Mexican Indians—is evident in a recent experiment conducted by a young man in the Southwest who fed LSD–25 to his marijuana (*Cannabis indica*) plants. Four plants were grown from seeds under identical conditions. The plants grew to about three inches in height, at which time he placed 500 micrograms of LSD–25 (in tab form) next to the roots of two of the plants, at a depth of two inches. Through watering, the LSD soon dissolved, and the effect on the two treated plants became immediately visible. The plants which had been given the LSD became a darker, richer green in color; the leaves became more symmetrical and had a crisper and more vital appearance. By the end of a few months, the "acid" pot plants were 50 percent larger than the other two plants. The experimenter reported that the two subject plants provided "a very fine smoke, with mild, short-duration hallucinatory experiences as previously encountered through the direct use of LSD–25."

LIKE AN EQUAL

Don Juan continued his lesson in *Journey to Ixtlan*. He points out that you can say anything to a plant, make up your own words. What is of importance is to treat the plant as an equal, to genuinely feel for it, to appreciate it. The existence of people and plants is circular: each in turn serves as food and sustenance for the other. Don Juan explains to his disciple that "a man who gathers plants must apologize every time for taking them and must assure them that some day his own body will serve as food for them." Once this larger picture is understood, neither people nor plants have more importance. We are even. To fully realize this notion, don Juan suggests that Castaneda talk to the plants, not so much for what he may say to them, but as an exercise in losing self-importance, an exercise through which he can enter into equality with the plants.

BETH CANNON

OLD DRYAD REMINISCENCES

Talk to your plants, but also listen. Learn from your plants. Meditate on you plants. As Walt Whitman noted, while walking through the trees, "How strong, vital, enduring! How dumbly eloquent! What suggestions of imperturbability and *being*, as against the human trait of mere *seeming*. Then the qualities, almost emotional, palpably artistic, heroic of a tree; so innocent and harmless, yet so savage. It *is*, yet says nothing. Science (or rather half-way science) scoffs at reminiscence of dryad and hamadryad, and of trees speaking. But if they don't, they do as well as most speaking, writing, poetry, sermons, or rather they do a great deal better. I should say indeed that these old dryad reminiscences are quite as true as any, and profounder than most reminiscences we get. Go and sit in a grove or woods, with one or more of those voiceless companions, and read the foregoing and think."

THE PLANT MEN

We have traveled into the past and paused briefly in the present to examine our common heritage with plants. Now, from Olaf Stapledon's *The Star-Maker*, we look at one interpretation of the future: "The typical plant man was an erect organism, like ourselves. On his head he bore a vast crest of green plumes, which could be either folded together in the form of a huge, tight, cos lettuce, or spread out to catch the light. Three many-faceted eyes looked out from under the crest. Beneath these were three arm-like manipulatory limbs, green and serpentine, branching at their extremities. The slender trunk, pliable, encased in hard rings which slid into one another as the body bowed, was divided into three legs for locomotion. Two of the three feet were also mouths, which could either draw sap from the root or devour foreign matter. The third was an organ of excretion. The precious excrement was never wasted, but passed through a special junction between the third foot and the root. The feet contained taste organs, and also ears. Since there was no air, sound was not propagated above the ground."

AN ECSTASY

The description of the plant men of the future is similar to mythological descriptions of the plant gods of the past. Another description of their existence resembles that state to which we might all, in our plant consciousness, wish to attain. "The state of the plant men did not consist merely of being united as a group mind, whether of tribe or race. The plant man did not in his daytime life come into possession of the percepts and thoughts of his fellow plant men, and thereby awaken into a more comprehensive and discriminate awareness of the environment and of the multiple body of the race. On the contrary, he became completely unresponsive to all objective conditions save the flood of sunlight drenching his spread leaves. And this experience afforded him an enduring ecstasy whose quality was almost sexual, an ecstasy in which subject and object seemed to become identical, an ecstasy of subjective union with the obscure source of all finite being."

THE TRANSPARENT EYEBALL

We live among plants. We receive their wisdom and mystique as people have done in simple and complex times, in past and present realms. Our perceptions are akin to those of Ralph Waldo Emerson, who wrote the following lines while meditating on his garden. "We return to reason and faith. There I feel that nothing can befall me in life, no disgrace, no calamity, which nature cannot repair. Standing on the bare ground, my head bathed by the blithe air, and uplifted into infinite space, all mean egotism vanishes. I become a transparent eyeball; I am nothing; I see all; the currents of the universal being circulate through me; I am part or particle of God."

PLANT CARE

This section of the book, "Plant Care," is the planet-side version of "Plant Consciousness." In reality, they are the same thing. One goes with the other. To equate "plant consciousness" with an ancient and innate spirituality and brotherhood with plants is to recognize that "plant care" is the language through which this communication takes place. As a language there is nothing mystical about it. The basics of plant care, the "how-to," must be learned, practiced, or even better, experienced.

Plant care involves nothing less than a serious commitment to the health and lives of the plants in our apartments and homes. The plants have been removed from their natural habitats, potted in individual containers, and brought into environmental circumstances alien to their normal growth patterns. In natural settings they adapt to the best and the worst of situations. In modern dwellings they are at our mercy. Nothing less than our heartfelt love and care will do.

So, while we talk to our plants, work out their astrological charts, play them music, and meditate amongst them, we must also make a daily commitment of mind, heart, time, and hard work. We must know their needs and requirements and attend to them. For only through these simple activities can the dialogue really begin.

A NEW ENVIRONMENT

The original growing conditions of the plants we bring into our homes are as diverse as the dryness of the desert and the humidity of the rain forest. Whatever species of plant is brought into the home, it must adjust to the conditions of our climate-controlled way of life. To satisfy its needs, it is essential that we know its original home, the conditions under which it grows best, and how these factors relate to its new environment.

The environments from which house plants originate can be conveniently classified as follows:

Desert: Intense daily sunshine, minimal rain, low humidity, and temperatures varying from high during the day to low at night. Many house plants originate in the deserts of the southwestern United States, Mexico, South America, the Middle East, and Australia.

Agave (Century Plant)
Cactus
Opunita (Bunny Ears)
Pereskia (Lemon Vine)

Subtropics: Short winter with lowest temperature of about forty degrees, and long summer with warm, sunny days. High humidity and regular rain throughout the year. Many plants in our homes originate in India, China, Japan, South Africa, and the southern United States.

Acouis (Chinese Sweet Flag)
Asparagus Fern
Aspidistra (Cast Iron Plant)
Begonia
Chlorophytum (Spider Plant)
Coleus
Cordyline (Ti-Plant)
Fatsia (Aralia)
Ficus (Fig Rubber Plant)
Gynura (Royal Velvet Plant)
Hedera (Ivy)
Hibiscus
Hypoestis
Maranta (Prayer Plant)
Olea (Olive)
Pittosporum
Pleomele

Rhoe (Moses-in-a-Boat)
Schefflera (Australian Umbrella Tree)
Succulents

BETH CANNON

Tropics: Steady heat and humidity. Light is often filtered through higher layers of foliage, and the soil consists of a layer of spongy and partially decayed vegetation. Strange as it seems, tropical plants that originate in the hot, steamy sections of South America and Africa are the easiest to grow in modern homes and apartments.

Abutilon (Flowering Maple)
Aglaonema (Chinese Evergreen)
Anthurium (Tail Flower)
Brassaia (Umbrella Tree)
Bromeliads
Caladium
Cissus

Codiaeum (Croton)
Columnea
Cyperius (Sedge)
Ferns
Dieffenbachia (Dumb Cane)
Dizygotheia (Finger Aralia)
Dracena
Episcia
Monstera (Swiss Cheese Plant)
Palms
Pandanus (Screw Pine)
Philodendron
Pilea
Spathiphyllum
Syngonium (Nephthytis)
Violet
Wandering Jew

Hybrids: These plants are produced by crossing two species. They are very adaptable to indoor environments because of their vitality and strength.

BUYING A HOUSE PLANT

Buying a house plant is first and foremost a question of the individual needs and requirements of the plant in regard to the right combination of light, heat, moisture, and so on. Don't buy a plant unless it will be living in an environment in which it can flourish. Check the plant with the New Environment list. If it is not on the list, check with the plant store for information about its original home.

Plants have a way of getting used to their owners, or rather, they readily adapt to a consistent pattern. Change is not appreciated. It is a good idea to buy plants in the spring and summer months when they can gradually adjust to their new world before being subjected to heat and artificial lighting during the colder weather. It is also important to realize that many plant stores and greenhouses are excessively humid. The shock of moving a plant from such conditions to a dry winter apartment can cause death by shock.

The following checklist indicates trouble signs to be avoided in purchasing a particular plant:

1 leaves with brown edges

2 yellow or faded lower leaves

3 leaves growing too far apart and/or roots coming out of the drainage holes or the surface of the soil

4 new leaves smaller than older ones

5 insects or signs of insects

An excellent ceremony for welcoming a new plant is a bath. Fill a sink with very warm water and mild soap flakes, such as Ivory Snow. Cover the soil with a cloth or paper, turn the plant upside down, and gently dunk it into the water. A brief soaking, swishing the foliage through the water, is helpful in preventing pests. Another effective measure is to soak the pot in water and drain well, thus removing the excess salts usually caused by overfertilization in the greenhouse.

It's a good idea to transplant new plants into soil mixtures. Check the general section on Soil, or, if indicated, the sections on Bromeliads, Cacti and Succulents, and Flowering Plants.

Commitment to the new plant is paramount. On the day it is purchased, and every day thereafter, check the plant carefully and determine and satisfy its needs.

The following information will be of use to any be-ginning indoor gardener:

☐ The key to growing houseplants is to raise them under conditions suitable for the individual plant. The energy level of the plant depends on photosyn-thesis, the process by which the leaves produce sugar and starches as food for the entire plant. If the right conditions are not met, this process is hampered and the energy level of the plant becomes low. The result will be weak colors, small leaves, and no growth.

☐ If the leaves turn brown at the tips, check for over-watering.

☐ If the leaves curl, the air in the apartment or home is probably too dry.

☐ If leaves drop off, it may be from cold drafts, not enough fertilizing, or insufficient humidity.

☐ If the leaves turn yellow or pale, the first thing to do is to check the roots. Knock the root ball out of the pot and check the color of the roots. If they are white, the roots are fine and the problem may be a lack of iron or the need to repot. If the root color is brown, the plant is dead, and the likely cause is too much water.

☐ If the leaves have yellow or brown patches, or if a cactus becomes yellow, there is too much light.

☐ On the other hand, if the leaves are far apart and become pale, or if a cactus looks weak and sluggish, there is not enough light.

☐ Brown tips on ferns are usually the result of the plant being bruised.

☐ Allow yellowed leaves to fall off by themselves. Before the leaf falls, the plant will begin to heal itself by sealing the spot where it was attached, lessening the possibility of infection.

☐ Don't expose plants to drafts.

☐ Avoid placing ripening apples around plants. They give off ethylene gas which can cause yellow foliage. The banana plant gives off the same chemical, one which can eventually kill other plants.

☐ Plants don't like most chemicals or vapors. The slightest traces of gas from a kitchen stove is deadly to most plants.

☐ All plants benefit from a gentle circulation of air.

☐ If new growth is very fast, but the plant seems to wilt and the pot has a white salty crust on it, chances are that the plant is being overfertilized.

☐ It is necessary to repot plants regularly, or the plant which has outgrown its pot will begin to shed its lower leaves. Most varieties of healthy plants have leaves going down to the bottom of the stem.

☐ Protect plants from cold winter nights. Leaves can get frostbitten if they touch cold windowpanes. It is sometimes necessary to place a plastic sheet between the plants and the window. In any event, always pull down shades at night during the winter.

☐ During the days, in both winter and summer, turn plants regularly so the good sides do not always face the light.

☐ Proper spacing is beneficial to the health of plants. Plants should not touch one another. When crowded too closely together, they can deteriorate.

☐ If many plants are desired, place them at different levels on top of clear jars, glass bricks, or plastic tubes. These transparent display pieces allow light to shine through on the smaller plants in front.

☐ Vacation time is a period in which plants can briefly take care of themselves. Water and cover them with plastic bags. Use bags from the dry cleaners for large plants. Tuck the open portion under the pot, not the saucer. When placed out of direct sunlight, the bag will function as a terrarium. If the pot has no drainage hole, water the plant, cover with a plastic bag, but wrap the open end loosely around the stem of the plant and tie in place. Moisture will then drop into the soil.

☐ Plants are uncomfortable in circumstances and situations uncomfortable for people. Keep this in mind, and by all means, use your intuition when caring for plants.

SOIL

Soil is the home, the immediate physical environment, of the plant. Its roots are confined to a small space and must be compatible with the condition of the soil. The soil, or a similar growing medium, provides physical support for the roots of a plant, and through it the plant receives water, nutrients, and oxygen. The soil must be in good condition: it must contain decayed organic material which holds moisture and aids in keeping the soil open so that oxygen can pass through, and it must be porous to allow water to pass through freely.

Soil Environment

Plants in their original habitats live in differing soil environments.

Desert plants need mostly coarse sand which allows water to penetrate rapidly to a considerable depth.

Tropical plants grow well in completely soilless mediums such as sphagnum moss or decayed leaf mold. Root systems are sparse. They also live in crevices of trees and derive nourishment from decaying matter.

Subtropical plants are found in clay, coarse sand, and silt with varying degrees of well-rotted matter or humus. These soils retain less water than a jungle floor. Such plants have complete root systems.

Soil Elements

The following elements are necessary for good plant growth: nitrogen, phosphorous, potash, calcium, sulphur, magnesium, iron, copper, zinc, boron, manganese, sodium, and aluminum. Nitrogen, phosphorous, and potash are particularly important for the soil of indoor plants. Nitrogen aids in the green-coloring chlorophyll process and promotes the growth of leaves and plant shoots. An overdose of nitrogen has a negative effect on cell development and flower production. Phosphorous stiffens the stems of plants, helps flowering and root growth, and aids in the production of fruits and seeds. Potash retards hyperactive growth and builds the plants resistance to disease. Potash can be added to soil that does not require acid by using wood ash, lime (which has an alkalinizing action), and fertilizers.

Pre-packaged Potting Soil

The base for most potting soil is loam, which is a combination of clay, silt, and sand. Sandy loam contains a larger proportion of sand. Loam is available in varieties of prepackaged potting soil at most plant and hardware stores. This is better for plants than outdoor soil because it has been pasteurized, thus lessening the chance of contamination by pests, fungi, or disease. There is less chance of stray seeds and roots, thus lessening the possibility of other growths in the pot. This kind of soil is all-purpose. It can be used in almost all circumstances, with modifications to meet specific needs. Many gardeners use compost, which is decomposed vegetable matter (grass, weeds, and leaves) with soil mixed in. Apartment gardeners may use all-purpose soil as compost.

Soil Additives

Various ingredients can be used to modify prepackaged soils for a particular plant.

Leaf mold is made from flaky, textured decayed leaves. It provides rich sources of health for houseplants. Making leaf mold is a long and involved process and is not practical for people living in apartments.

Peat moss is the carbonized residue of sphagnum moss which has been decomposed under water or in a bag. It is high in acid and aids in stimulating additional growth from root hairs and in increasing the capacity of the soil to retain moisture.

Bone meal is one of the original fertilizers. It breaks down slowly, keeps the plant healthy for a long period of time, provides an organic source of phosphorous, and does not burn the root hairs.

Perlite is a pelletized, porous white volcanic rock which absorbs many times its own weight in water. It aids in supplying oxygen to the roots by making soil lighter and avoiding packing.

Vermiculite helps keep soil from getting too hard. Most all-purpose soils already have this additive, which is made out of mica rock subjected to intense heat.

Builder's sand consists of coarse, sharp particles that have been cleaned of soil and seeds. This is not ordi-

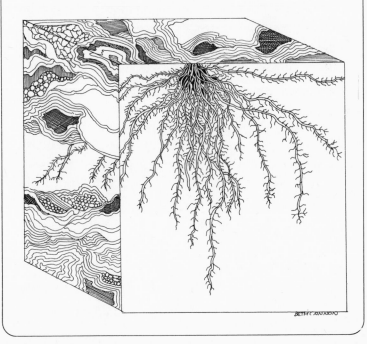

BETH CANNON

nary smooth, salty beach sand, but the kind used for making mortar. The grit it provides to the soil allows air space by making tiny pockets in the earth around which air forms. It also promotes drainage. No matter how well a plant is nourished, it will not stay alive if it lacks the proper amount of air.

Sphagnum moss is a bog plant that protects young plants from disease. Sometimes it is used alone for growing bromeliads and other epiphytes. Shredded bark and osmunda fiber are also used for growing epiphytes.

Agricultural charcoal is useful in filtering out additives and pollutants in tap water. Place a layer on the top of the potted soil.

Soil Mixtures

An excellent mixture for nearly all house plants is made of equal amounts of all-purpose soil (with vermiculite), peat moss or leaf mold, and builder's sand. A pinch of limestone helps counteract the acidity of the peat moss.

Some plants, such as philodendrons, require a highly organic mixture. Mix together equal amounts of peat moss or plant mold and perlite or vermiculite.

For cacti and succulents, mix together equal amounts

of all-purpose soil (with vermiculite) and builder's sand.

For gardenias, azaleas, and other organic soil plants, mix together equal amounts of all-purpose soil (with vermiculite) and leaf mold, sphagnum moss, or peat moss, and add a handful of sand. These plants prefer the more acid soil which peat moss can give them.

Whatever the mixture, be sure it is moist, not dry or wet. Tender roots suffer less damage in moist soil. Soils and peat are usually moist when purchased. They keep well when sealed in plastic bags.

Use agricultural charcoal on top of the potted soil, or the top will become packed and hard from watering. Another problem is possible algae growth. If the soil does become packed, loosen it with a pointed stick or a fork.

FERTILIZERS

Consider fertilizer as an aid to healthy plant growth, rather than as a remedy for damage or "illness." Many of the soil elements necessary for plant growth may be washed away by water. House plant fertilizers are water soluble and contain nutrient elements in an inorganic form that plants can use immediately. Fertilizers can be very helpful to plants grown in soil; they are a necessity for plants grown in sphagnum moss and other soilless mediums.

Do not feed a plant for at least four or five months after buying it, and never feed foliage plants more than once every few months. Even then, plants potted in fertile soil do not need additional fertilizer until the pot becomes crowded with roots. Bone meal is often placed at the bottom of a pot and feeds the plant for months. In any event, leave plants alone if they are growing well. Never give fertilizer to a plant that is suffering from overwatering; the additional nutrients will only add to its troubles.

Start fertilizing during the spring, when the plants show signs of active growth after the long winter months. Read labels and follow directions carefully. Always use a slightly weaker solution than suggested in the directions. Frequent fertilizing makes plants grow too big and too fast. At a certain point they have to be either cut back or thrown away. Never feed a foliage plant that is in dormancy. Fertilization during this time can disturb natural growth rhythms.

Many commercial fertilizers supply the optimum 1:2:1 proportion of nitrogen, phosphorous, and potassium. For additional potassium, cigar and cigarette ash can be used. The inner membrane of eggshells is also a good fertilizer. Soak the eggshells overnight in water and use the water on the plants.

Plants grown under artificial lights use the fertilizer recommended for other house plants.

The key to the choice of pots is proper drainage. Good drainage allows the spaces in the soil to be filled with air rather than water, permitting the plant to "breathe" oxygen which is necessary for its life. Poor drainage results in a lack of oxygen and overwatering, both of which can kill a plant.

Plastic vs. Clay Pots

Plastic pots are gaining in popularity. The advantage the plastic pot has over the traditional red clay pot is that plants do not have to be watered as often. The disadvantage is the risk of overwatering because of reduced evaporation.

Neither air nor water can pass through the sides of the nonporous plastic pot. Evaporation, which activates the roots and keeps soil in good condition, can occur only through the top of the soil. Surplus moisture can escape only through drainage holes, and excess salts in the soil, which seep through the sides of clay pots, have no escape in plastic pots. Good drainage in plastic pots is particularly important. One helpful practice is to place more crocked material over the drainage holes in plastic pots.

Plants in plastic pots need half as much watering as plants in clay pots. On balance, it is better to water more often and stick with the clay pot.

Flexible Plastic

These rubberlike pots can damage the roots resting against them and should be avoided. Also, the material from which these pots are made is toxic to plants. Styrofoam pots are very lightweight and fall over easily. Air, but not water, can pass through the porous surface.

Hanging Pots

Special hanging pots made from plastic consist of a pot with an attached saucer to catch excess water. These pots usually have their own hanging hook.

Local hardware stores carry chains in a variety of sizes and strengths, which are sold by the foot. Clay pots are still preferable. Special nets, which vary from simple heavy twine to elaborate macramé designs, are available for hanging both a clay pot and a separate saucer. The nets are hung from a ceiling hook, and the pot and saucer are placed inside.

For large plants and trees, use large square or round wooden tubes.

WATER

Green plants make their own food by turning light energy into carbohydrates. Water is essential for photosynthesis; it provides carbon, hydrogen, and oxygen. Drowning a healthy plant is a frequent mistake. Plants do well in damp, but not wet, soil. Overwatering forces out the air that the roots use for respiration. The root hairs at the bottom of the pot absorb moisture from the surface. Root hairs are the backbone of every plant system—only they absorb moisture. Water must flow through the pot to the bottom. Be sure that the excess water flows through the drainage holes.

The water should not drain out too quickly. The soil must be thoroughly soaked. When the water drains too fast, the soil around the root ball has become too dry and has shrunk away from the sides, and the water bypasses the root hairs. If this is the case, take the entire pot, dunk it in a sink or tubful of water, and leave it there until bubbles stop coming up from the soil. Then take the pot out and let it drain well. Never let a pot sit in drained water for more than an hour. Pour it out.

Time must be allowed between waterings for air to permeate the soil. Different species dry out at different speeds. Some, such as succulents, can survive a long time without moisture. Their water is stored in their thick leaves and stems. To determine when to water, stick a finger into the soil, about one and one-half inches down. If the soil is dry, it is time to water.

Water plants in the morning, while the temperature is rising. The need for water is greatest during the day, and it is best for the plant not to have wet soil when the temperature is falling. Water less when plants are dormant, even if the soil is dry and under normal circumstances it would be time to water. Small pots dry out faster and need more frequent watering than large ones. Hanging plants need more water than a plant in the ground.

Use warm water on almost all plants; cold water can cause wilting and retarded growth. Cold water also harms cells in the leaves of African violets and other gesneriads and causes yellow spots on their leaves. Do not use softened water, which contains chemicals that can kill plants. If the tap water is so heavily chlorinated that there is a noticeable odor, pour the water into a watering can and allow it to stand overnight, the chlorine will evaporate. Put an ice cube on the edge of the pot of a hanging plant in the summer. It melts slowly and keeps the plant moist.

Watering is part science, part art. A certain familiarity with individual plants, as well as a store of past experience in such matters, will be most helpful.

HUMIDITY

Humidity is a measure of moisture in the air. With regard to house plants, it affects the rate of transpiration, the process by which water from the interior of the leaves and the stems escapes through the plant's pores and evaporates into the air. When there is a lack of humidity, the water evaporates too quickly, resulting in wilted stems and leaves.

It is essential to have enough humidity around house plants. Dry air can kill them. Remember that cool spots are more humid than warm spots. The very worst place for a plant is in the path of hot air coming from a radiator. Plants grouped together (but not touching) will create a synergistic effect and raise the humidity of the area by transpiring around each other's foliage and adding extra moisture to the air.

There are several other ways to increase humidity. Try placing a layer of damp pebbles in waterproof trays under the pots. The pebbles should be about two inches deep, and the tray should be filled with water up to, but not touching, the bottom of the pot. A portable humidifier can raise humidity quite a bit. This is essential in steam-heated apartments during the winter—for both plants and people.

An essential humidity-raising technique is to spray-mist the plants each day. Think of it as a morning wake-up ritual. Find a sprayer that produces a fine mist without leaving excessive amounts of water on the leaves. Spray both on top and under the leaves.

If a plant's leaves curl after spraying, the room is probably too dry and the water thus evaporates too quickly. If this is the case, spray all around the plant instead of directly on the leaves. Don't spray plants with fuzzy leaves, cacti, and succulents. Don't forget to spray the roots of climbing plants that use moisture to help them get a firm grip.

Allow the water used for spraying to sit overnight. The chlorine will evaporate, and the water will reach room temperature, which gives best results in spraying plants.

Wash plants once or twice a month. One method is to take a shower with them. Spray occasionally with hot water and mild soap flakes to help keep bugs away.

Don't leave soap on the plants. After the soap and water solution dries, rinse with warm water. A weak solution of tea is also an effective antiseptic. Wash fuzzy-leaved plants regularly by covering the soil with a cloth and dunking the foliage in a tub or sink of warm water and mild soap flakes. This helps keep bugs away. Rinse with room-temperature water.

Never use leaf shiners. They collect dust, block pores, and suffocate the plant.

If a plant is not drying out properly, check the drainage holes to see if they're clogged. Push a stick or a pencil through the drainage hole. If nothing is in the way, it is necessary to repot.

LIGHT

Light is the source of energy for all plant growth. The photosynthesis which takes place during the day is not possible at night when the carbohydrates created through light energy are turned into sugar to develop cells and tissues. To do this they need the stimulus of a drop in temperature at the end of the day. House plants are usually near windows, where it is cooler at night.

The intensity of light is the major determinant of the growth rate of plants. The best light is during the summer, when the sun is high in the sky and covers the shortest distance from earth. During the winter, the sun is lower in the sky and is diffused and deflected by atmospheric interferences.

Be very careful about giving plants the proper amount of light. A plant can live a long time on stored-up light energy. By the time it is dying from too little light, it will be too late to save it.

Place plants in an area that gets at least a few hours of filtered sunlight each day. Cacti do best in direct sun. Use large plants to shade young plants. Move plants gradually from shady to sunny spots. Whenever such a move is necessary, give them two weeks to adjust properly.

When plants are not getting enough light, two things often happen: the lower leaves die and the new leaves are small. A south window will get the most sun. An east window will get the morning light, which provides the most life-giving rays. Lamp-lit corners (with white walls) can be a good source of light. In any light, always rotate plants around every few days to insure even distribution.

Artificial Lighting

Artificial lighting is most useful during the winter months. Special plant lights use red and blue radiant energy from the opposite ends of the color spectrum. The red light stimulates vegetative growth; the blue light affects the regulatory system. These lights are necessary because normal sunlight is sometimes not sufficient during winter and ordinary incandescent lights create excessive heat and are weak in the red and blue bands. It is often imperative to use the fluorescent tubes and spotlights that have been designed particularly for indoor plant gardening.

In normal light (but no sun), use two 100-watt lights placed on the corners of a window frame. If there is no daylight, place plant lights 8 inches above the soil for seedlings, and 15 inches above the foliage of older plants. If long tube lights are used, plants needing the most light should be in the center, and plants needing less light should be at the ends.

Leave plant lights on for 12 to 16 hours. For best results, do this at the same time each day. If this is impractical, buy a timer to do the chore automatically.

PROPAGATION

Plants can be propagated by two basic methods. The first involves vegetative procedures, such as cuttings, offshoots, divisions, and runners. The second is starting from scratch with seeds. With either method it is best to use red clay pots, which allow air to pass through their porous sides and which provide proper drainage. Coffee cans may also be used if a hole is drilled in the bottom. A one-quart milk carton, cut down and with a hole punched through the bottom, may also serve as a pot. Whatever the container, it must not be more than two or three inches round. The best time of year to propagate is spring or early summer.

Seeds

Use fresh seeds. This can be a problem because many fruits and vegetables are pasteurized to prevent spoilage, and preservatives are often added. These seeds will not germinate. Take the following steps in planting seeds:

1 Soak the clay pots for a few hours so they become thoroughly wet and won't absorb moisture from the soil.

2 Prepare a soilless medium of sphagnum moss, vermiculite, and perlite. A soilless medium prevents "damping off," which is a bacteria that can cause diseased plants or prevent the seeds from germinating.

Fill to rim of the pot, and with the heel of the hand, press the soil down to one inch below rim.

3 Wet the surface and sprinkle with seeds.

4 Cover large seeds to twice their diameter with vermiculite or fine sphagnum moss to keep them moist during germination, which can take from several days to several weeks.

5 Water by setting the pot into a sinkful of room-temperature water. Leave it in the water until the surface of the medium is moist. Do not water from the top. Remove the pot and let it drain. Place a plastic bag over the pot and tuck the bottom under the pot. Place it in bright light until seedlings begin to emerge. The seeds of tropical plants need heat to germinate, and this heat should come from underneath. The soil must be kept moist.

6 When the seedlings emerge, remove the plastic bags and care for the needs of the seedlings according to their species. Keep the soil moist during the day by watering in the morning. The soil will dry by night.

7 The leaves of new seedlings will not look like those of the species. When the leaves appear, pry up the seedlings with a spoon, taking the soil around roots with it, and transplant into two-inch pots, using a soil mixture of equal parts of sharp sand or gravel, peat, and all-purpose soil. Plastic bags are useful to contain the mosture necessary for youthful growth.

8 As soon as the young plant becomes root-bound, re-pot in a container no more than two sizes larger than the first pot. Use the appropriate growing medium for the species.

Growing Ferns From Spores

Ferns do not have seeds. The reproductive organs are small spores, tiny particles in a casing which is found underneath the leaves and is in evidence from spring to early fall. Follow these steps in reproducing a fern from spores:

1 Prepare the pots and growing medium, as with seeds. The proper mixture is builder's sand (one part), all-purpose soil (two parts), and peat moss (two parts).

2 When a spore case ripens, remove a leaf and place it in a paper bag until the case dries out and disintegrates (usually one week). Empty the contents and remove everything except the dust-like brown spores. Sprinkle the spores across surface of the potting soil.

3 Water the pot and place it in plastic bag, as with seeds. It must be kept moist.

4 Within a few days to a year, the surface of the growing medium will become covered with a green slime. Heart-shaped growth will appear. When it grows to one-quarter of an inch in diameter, it will

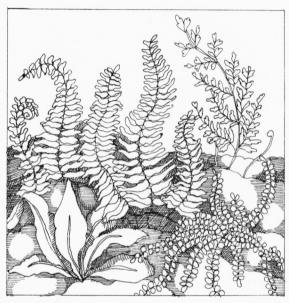

produce female and male organs on its undersides. As they grow, the male organ releases sperm which swim through the slime to the egg cells.

5 Remove the plastic bag when the plants are about one and one-half inches tall. Lift a few plants out together on a spoon and plant them in small pots with a mixture of equal parts of all-purpose soil and peat moss.

6 Water according to species. In about a year, separate the clumps and plant them individually in soil appropriate for the species.

Rooting Cuttings

Any plant that has a stem or branches can be propagated through cuttings. Some of the species best propagated by this method are tropical plants, philodendrons, ivy, and geraniums.

1 Cut off a two-inch piece of stem with at least two leaves attached. Cut the stem one-quarter inch below the leaf joint, or node. Remove the leaves from the section that will be below the surface of the rooting medium.

2 Wrap all but the newly cut end in a wet paper towel until the cut end dries, about one hour. Cacti and succulents need to stay dry for several days.

3 Use a moistened medium, such as a combination of sand, peat moss, sphagnum moss, and vermiculite. Most cuttings root in water but are not durable and transplantable to a new home.

4 Make a one-inch hole in the medium with a stick or pencil. Insert the cutting and firm the medium around it. Plant several cuttings in one pot. Give the plants a thorough soaking with water. Cover with a plastic bag, tuck the end under the pot, and place in bright light with no sun.

5 After two weeks, check the roots by pulling up a cutting. If the roots are not one to two inches in length, stick the cutting back into the medium and

wait. When the roots are the right length, they are ready for their own pots and the proper soil for their species. Use small pots for young plants, and plant at the same depth at which it stood in the rooting medium. This can be seen in the color of the stem, which will be darker in color above ground level.

6 Return the plant to the place where it rooted. Spray frequently, and after a week, move it to the best location for the species.

Leaf Cuttings

Some of the species that can be grown from a single leaf are African violets, rex begonias, and many succulents.

1 The stem of a leaf cutting is inserted in the rooting medium, which is sand or the mixture used for stem cuttings. The leaf itself is left exposed. If the leaf is stemless or has a short stem, its base is partially buried.

2 A plant will develop beneath the rooting medium, and the leaf itself will eventually die. Use the root-cutting method from this point. The length of time for rooting can be a month or longer.

Dividing

Plants sending up a dense thicket of green stem growth at the soil level can be divided into two or

146

more plants, each part retaining part of the original root system and top growth. Plants that cannot be divided are vining, trailing, and climbing species.

1 Cut down on watering for a few days to make the plant tougher and less vulnerable.

2 Knock off the pot and shake off the soil.

3 Some plants will fall apart. If one does not, use a sharp knife and cut through the crown of the plant, the area where roots and top growth are joined.

4 Immediately repot each plant in the appropriate medium.

5 Water thoroughly. Give the plant light but no sun. Cut back the foliage severely to encourage new growth. Do not water until the soil feels dry to the touch.

Air Layering

In this method new roots are grown while they are still attached to the parent plant. This approach works best for the rubber plant, dracena, and other one-stemmed plants which lose so much moisture from their leaf surfaces that they would wilt before roots form if the other propagation methods were attempted.

1 Cut a notch one-third to one-half the way through the stem, just below a node.

2 Wrap the stem with a large double handful of moist moss and tie it firmly in place. Keep it constantly moist.

3 Wrap the moss in plastic to prevent loss of water by evaporation, leaving an opening in the plastic so that water can be added to the moss as needed.

4 Roots will form in two to five months. Cut off the layer and pot in the appropriate medium without disturbing the moss which surrounds the roots. Water according to the species.

Layering

Plants that behave as vines can be propagated by bending the long stems back over the rim of the pot and laying them horizontally directly on the potting medium. Keep moist. After the roots have formed, cut the stem in sections. The roots and shoot formed at each node are the start of a new plant.

Runners

Some house plants send out aerial runners which form new plants on their ends. Such plants are easily propagated by bringing the ends of the runner in contact with moist soil. It soon takes root and grows. At this point, cut it off and propagate the same as root cuttings.

Suckers and Offshoots

Some plants, such as bromeliads, produce small stem-less replicas that grow out from its base or stem. Cut these off with a sharp knife when they are four inches tall and repot individually (the same as root cuttings) in three-inch pots. When roots become pot-bound, place in a five-inch pot. This size holds the new plant and its offshoots for three years. The new plants usually flower one or two years after separation. The original plant does not bloom again.

REPOTTING

Repotting is necessary when the root system extends throughout the soil, filling the spaces between the particles and interfering with normal growth and development. A plant is ready for repotting when (1) the foliage wilts in spite of normal watering, (2) the plant sheds its lowest leaves or they turn yellow and die, (3) the leaves fail to develop to their normal size, or (4) the roots protrude out of the drainage holes.

Some plants can be repotted at any time; others, preferring to be root-bound, don't have to be repotted at all. Many large plants do not have to be repotted. Just remove two inches of soil from the surface and add new soil. This adds nutrients and removes salt that has accumulated from watering and fertilizers.

Before repotting a plant, make sure that it actually is root-bound. Place your hand over the top of the pot, turn the plant upside down, and gently tap the rim against a table or wrap a towel around a hammer and tap the pot all around until the root ball falls out. It should fall out in a solid lump. If a mass of roots presses closely against the wall of the pot and there is no loose soil, it is time to repot.

It is important to note that the roots of plants die before the foliage. When the roots are in poor condition (when they are brown instead of a healthy white), discard the plant because a dying plant will affect the healthy plants around it.

July and August are the best months for repotting. Plants are in active growth and can best adapt to change.

Use a pot no more than two inches wider than the root ball. Overpotted plants become waterlogged and are usually unhealthy. There are not enough roots to quickly use up the water. The two inches of extra room supplied by the new pot is enough for a year's growth.

Thoroughly scrub and sanitize any used pot with germicidal soap, steel wool, and hot water. Clean away salts and sticking roots and dry the pot before using, or the soil will cling to the sides.

Proper drainage is important. If water accumulates at the bottom of the pot, the roots will rot. Place broken pieces of clay pots across the drainage hole, concave side down, and add a layer of gravel. In a holeless container, use a minimum of one inch of gravel on the bottom. A good drainage pot can be inserted inside a holeless container by surrounding the space between the pots with sphagnum moss.

1 Prepare the soil mixture ahead of time so that the root ball does not dry out during the transplanting process. Make sure the soil is damp.

2 Always water the plant the day before it is repotted so that the soil in the root ball is uniformly moist.

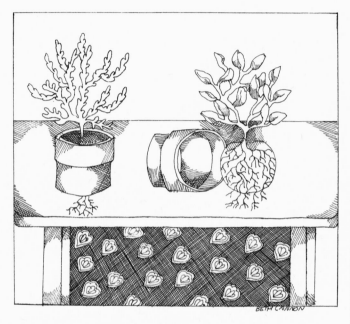

3 Knock the root ball out of the old pot by banging the pot against a table, or hit it lightly with a hammer wrapped in a towel. If the root ball does not fall out readily, the pot will have to be broken with a hammer.

4 If sphagnum moss is used, place a layer over the drainage material in the new pot to keep the soil from clogging the drainage channels. If soil is used pack two inches of soil firmly over the drainage material. Before inserting the plant, make a mold, fill the pot three-quarters full of soil, and press the soil firmly

against the sides of the pot. If the plant is being re-potted because it is unhealthy, remove all soil from the root ball. If it is healthy, put the root ball and the old soil into the new pot.

5 Center the plant in the new pot. The top of the root ball should be one-half inch below the top of the pot for proper maturing. Don't bury the original surface of the soil. The soil around the root ball must be firm. Apply pressure to the soil around the rim, and bang the pot hard on the floor to settle the soil.

6 Water thoroughly. The water should drain through the bottom. Prune slightly to help send energy to the roots. If a sensitive or damaged plant has been transplanted, cover the top portion with clear plastic and spray several times a day to prevent excessive wilting. When the root hairs grow out, they will absorb an adequate amount of water and the plastic can then be removed.

GROOMING

Grooming improves the shape of a plant, helps develop strong flower-bearing shoots, and prevents a
plant from growing to an unwieldy size. Grooming
methods include pruning, pinching, and training.

Pruning

Pruning keeps plants from growing to an unwieldly
size, promotes good flower shoots, and improves the
shape. Succulents, plants that grow directly from the
soil, like ferns or spathiphyllums, and plants that grow
straight up must not be pruned.

Use a sharp knife, scissors, or pruning shears for pruning. Plants have small buds where the leaf stalks join
the stem. These develop into a branch only if the
terminal bud at the end of the growing shoots is removed. Make a cut just above the point where a new
branch is desired, at a place where there is a bud to
develop into a new leader. Cut only two or three
stems at one time so that the plant is not shocked.

Pinching

Do not pinch succulents as it will leave scars. Plants
growing straight up or directly from the soil, like ferns,
also cannot be pinched. When branches start to grow,
they can be induced to grow faster by pinching. With

your thumbnail and finger, remove the tip of a growing shoot. Bushy growth is thus promoted by stopping the growth of stray shoots and stimulating the shoot buds which otherwise might remain dormant. Also, pinching flower buds encourages more foliage.

Root Pruning

This method is used for keeping large plants in the same pot. Prune roots in the spring when growth is most vigorous and wounds heal quickly.

1 Water the plant the day before so that the soil is not too dry.

2 Knock the plant out of the pot.

3 Place the root ball on a hard surface, and with a sharp knife, quickly remove one third of the side roots.

4 Reshape the root mass to the form of the pot sides, that is, wider at the top, and repot.

5 Prune the foliage slightly and water thoroughly. Cover with a plastic bag tucked under the bottom of the pot and keep out of direct sunlight for a few weeks.

DORMANCY

Most plants have a partial or complete sleeping period, a time of inactivity during which all vital growth processes become inactive because of shorter days, less rain, or a fall in temperature. They need rest. If they are disturbed during this period, they will die of exhaustion. Normal care, such as regular watering, or fertilization, can kill a plant during this period.

Cacti and succulents should not be watered for one full month during the winter. Allow a few extra days between waterings for slow-growing plants: even more time between waterings for plants that show no growth.

BROMELIADS

Bromeliads, a relative of the pineapple, are an interesting and varied family of over 1,800 species. They grow in tropic regions. Most are epiphytes, or air plants, which grow on rocks and trees. Others, called terrestrial plants, grow in soil and survive with less attention than any other house plant. Their seeds are spread by birds that eat the fleshy material around the berries and wipe their beaks clean on nearby branches, thus implanting the seeds.

Always put bromeliads in small clay pots as their root systems are limited and need little space. Never surround the roots with wet soil, and water only when the soil is dry.

Some bromeliads have broad leaves, others are grass-like. The blooming flowers are carried in low clusters in the heart of plants or on tall spikes. Some carry their flowers in colorful flower heads. The flowers can last as long as six months. Place the plants in bright light, but shade from the hot sun. Keep the tubulars filled with water in order to have a healthy plant.

To make a potting mixture for epiphytes, mix together equal amounts of all-purpose soil, builder's sand, and peat moss, and add half that amount of crushed granite. A potting mixture for terrestials can be made of equal parts of leaf mold, manure, and builder's sand.

Regular soil mixes may be used if the pot is fast-draining and porous. Fertilizer is optional. Propagation usually is from offshoots.

CACTI AND SUCCULENTS

The succulent and cactus family consists of more than 6,000 water-storing plants, including many groups that grow in dry desert areas. The spiny varieties are known as cacti, the fleshy-stemmed varieties as succulents. The thick stems of the cacti function as leaves in the manufacture of food. Both cacti and succulents store water for long periods of time and adapt remarkably well to indoor conditions.

These plants do best in small pots. For round plants, use a pot one inch wider than the diameter of the plant. For tall, growing plants, select a pot half as wide as the plant is tall. Repot every two years during the spring months.

See the Soil Section for the type of soil to use in re-potting, but be sure to use a dry soil, one rich in organic matter, and include a great deal of gritty material. A special cacti mixture can be purchased at plant stores. Never bury the fleshy part of the stem for it will rot and eventually kill the plant. Never press the soil down around cacti roots. If the plant refuses to stand, anchor it with flat plant labels. Do not water young plants for a few days, but give them a light spray of water occasionally. Do not water thoroughly for at least two weeks.

Cacti need less watering than other plants. They can be watered once a month in winter and twice a month in summer. They like bright sunny places and need little humidity.

Succulents need a bright cool spot. Always scratch down an inch into the soil, and if dry, water thoroughly from the top. Never water on a time schedule. During the winter allow them a month without watering. Water when their leaves become wrinkled, which indicates that their inner supply of water is depleted.

Cacti and succulents are propagated with leaf cuttings or offshoots. Insert the cutting into a dry medium, such as builder's sand, and set in a warm shady spot until rooting takes place. Water just enough to keep the cutting from shriveling up.

FLOWERING PLANTS

The important thing to remember about flowering plants is that they bloom only when the light level approximates that of their natural habitat. African violets survive in bright northern light with no sun, and they bloom year-round. Other flowering plants, lacking bright light, need artificial light to be grown successfully.

Budded plants need a great deal of water, but plants in full bloom will keep their blooms longer if they are watered moderately. Never let the blooms die on the

plant. A dry bloom takes energy away from the rest of the plant.

Citrus plants are the most adaptable for blossoming under indoor growing conditions. Attractive winter plants, such as cyclamen and azaleas, need a cool location year-round.

Many outdoor plants, such as chrysanthemums and azaleas, are sold by florists and grocers and mistakenly are thought to be plants that can live indoors. Though they may look beautiful for a month or so, they can't be expected to live indoors indefinitely. Regard them as a lovely bouquet.

BULBS

Winter Bulbs

Plant winter bulbs in peat moss and aquarium charcoal, allowing twice the depth of the bulb for root space. Expose the upper half of the bulb. Regular waterings are necessary. Placed in a sunny window, the planted bulbs produce early flowers. When the flowers and leaves are dead, leave the bulbs in the pot. During this dormancy period, keep the bulbs in a warm, dry place. In the fall, when new life appears, begin watering once again. During the second year of bloom, dust the plant with dried cow manure.

Buy large, full bulbs, making sure they are covered with paper thin outer skins to protect from bruising. Don't buy bulbs that have already started to grow from the top. Keep them dry and cool until ready to plant. The best storage method is in a paper bag punched with holes and placed in the refrigerator.

Hyacinths are easy bulbs with which to begin. The bulbs are large and the foliage grows quite tall. Crocus bulbs also grow quickly (the indented bald portion is the bottom of the bulb and the portion with the hairy stem is the top). Plant amaryllis in rich soil and sand.

Spring Bulbs

Treat spring bulbs as plants and place them in containers with crocking and soil. Plant them with the tips of the bulbs showing at the top of the soil. Water regularly, but don't drench. They fall into a resting period during the winter and during the hot days of late July and August. Remove the flower buds and let the leaves grow. While they are resting, keep them in a dry, warm place, and don't water them. In the fall and spring, when new life appears, begin watering once again.

TERRARIUMS

Plants grown in terrariums exist in their own micro-climates, an environment providing them with much greater amounts of moisture than is common in the average home. A terrarium is a self-regulating system. The water given off by the leaves as vapor condenses on the container and drips down back to the roots.

Terrariums can be created from any number of covered glass containers, such as bowls, apothecary jars, wine bottles, or aquarium tanks. Whatever the container, it must be thoroughly clean.

Set up the terrarium as follows:

1 charcoal base

2 one inch of gravel for drainage

3 sufficient all-purpose soil to hold roots

4 line outside with moss

5 place small plants in front, large plants in the rear

6 Wet the dry plants after they are placed inside the terrarium.

Water condensation on the glass each night indicates moisture inside. If the glass becomes heavily coated with moisture, take the top off for a few hours. Replace it when the moisture is reduced to a fine mist of droplets on the glass.

If the system is in balance, it may not need water for months or years. The only time it needs to be watered

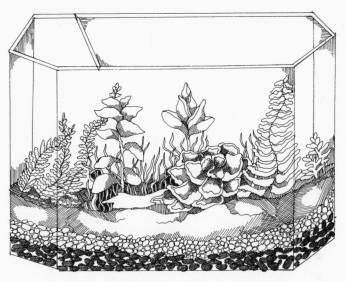

is if the edges of the moss crinkle or turn brown. Use fertilizer sparingly, for the plants quickly will outgrow the environment. After the first year, fertilize lightly every six months.

The best plants for terrariums are ferns, African violets, moss, small araliads, philodendrons, ivy, small palms, and begonias.

TRAINING AN INDOOR TREE

The following steps illustrate how to train an indoor tree, in this particular case, a coleus:

1 Start with a single stemmed six-inch plant in a small pot. Insert a foot-long stake and tie the stem loosely to it.

2 When the plant grows to ten inches, move the plant to a five-inch pot and insert a three-foot stake. Prune the twin-leaved side shoots.

3 Remove the flower spike and one side leaf and shoot. Tie the other leaf so its shoots form the growing tip.

4 When the tree is two feet in height, transplant it to an eight-inch pot, stake and all. For a three-foot tree, pinch off the central growing tip of the stem. As new shoots appear, pinch off the tips to encourage branching. After a year or two the stem may eventually stiffen enough to allow the removal of the stake.

The best defense against pests is good plant hygiene. Wash the leaves with a damp cloth at least once a month, especially larger-leaved plants. A shower is also helpful. Another method is to swish the foliage in warm water and mild soap flakes. If chemical sprays are used rinse the leaves with clear water after the chemical dries. A small amount of nicotine sulphate added to each gallon of soapy water helps a plant on which other methods have not worked. Read directions before using any insecticide.

Brown spots or curled brown edges can mean a fungus disease. Such diseases, along with mildew, can be controlled by specially formulated fungicide. However, throw away seriously diseased plants as they can spread disease to other plants.

Ants

Black, brown, and red ants are attracted to plants by insects that secrete honeydew. They injure roots and carry away seedlings.

Aphids

Aphids are sucking insects with soft, round or pear-shaped bodies. They come in many colors and usually cluster on new growth and buds, secreting a sticky liquid while sucking plant juices and causing poor growth.

Thrips

These barely visible slender insects are brown or black when mature, white and yellow when young. The adults fly and leap about plant leaves, sucking the juices from the tissues and disturbing the color and appearance of the leaves.

White Flies

These pests are very small and have white wings. The young attack the bottoms of the leaves, feed on the juices, and turn the leaves pale. The surfaces of the leaves become covered with honeydew.

Mites (Spider)

These flat, oval, red insects are found on the bottoms of leaves and are very hard to see. They turn leaves yellow before killing them. The plant itself becomes stunted.

Scales

There are many kinds of scales. Some have shell-like coverings and others have scales that cover the entire body. Some attack leaves, some attack stems, and some attack both. They suck the leaves, secrete honey-dew, and stunt plant growth.

Mealy Bugs

Mealy bugs are sucking insects that resemble tiny pieces of cotton. They clutter in leaf axils or in branch crotches, killing plants or slowing growth. The best way to combat them is by touching the bugs with alcohol on a cotton swab.

Mites (Cyclamen)

These oval bugs are too small to be visible to the naked eye. They attack young plants and buds. Blackening of infested parts is a common sign. Throw away any plant you think may be infested.

Nematodes

Nematodes are microscopic worms that attack roots and stunt growth. Throw away an infested plant.

Slugs and Earthworms

Slugs are shell-less snails that chew holes in leaves. Earthworms disturb root hairs. Bring them to the surface by watering the plant with a solution of one teaspoon of dry mustard to a gallon of water.